EDGEWOOD RESORT

EDGEWOOD RESORT
A Place Apart

Julie Schopieray

BACON PRESS
Cedar, Michigan

ISBN: 978-0-615-4626-3-9
Library of Congress Control Number: 2011904309

To order additional copies of this book, please contact the author at:

Bacon Press
3560 E. Gatzke Road
Cedar, Michigan 49621

or via email at: jschopieray@centurytel.net

PRINTED IN THE UNITED STATES OF AMERICA

Cover and text design by www.tothepointsolutions.com

CONTENTS

ACKNOWLEDGMENTS

I WOULD like to thank the following people who helped me put together this story of Edgewood Resort:

Betty (Craker) Armstrong, James B. Angell III, Liz and Peter Blick, Chris and Dick Cook, Monica Dillon, Kathleen Donnelly, Mary Ellis, Bernard Flickinger, Peggy Godwin, Marly Hanson, David Lathrop, Mary Liles, Judy McKinley-Braun, Jim Noller, Bernard Oakes, Al Raphelson, Rhea Sivek, Alice and Mary Thirlby, Todd Townley, Helen Vogel, and Mary Beth Wakulat.

Edgewood is not a place known to fame . . . It is a place apart; a place to which those worthy of it may come and rest awhile . . . Here are cool breezes in shady woodland nooks . . . under the pines, the scent of the cedars and hemlocks soothe tired brains and worn nerves. . . . The summing up of the whole matter is expressed in the words "It is good to be here."

~ from various articles published during the 1890s
in the *Grand Traverse Herald*

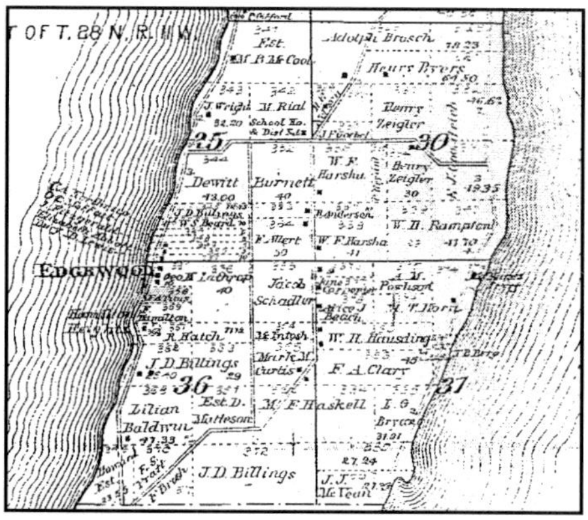

A map that indicates the land ownership at Edgewood. (1895)

THE BEGINNING

Along the western side of the Old Mission Peninsula in Grand Traverse County, people drive a small stretch of scenic road usually unaware that they are passing through what was once one of the most popular summer destinations in Northern Michigan: Edgewood Resort.

In 1883, George and Cornelia Lathrop purchased ten acres of land on the lower part of the Old Mission Peninsula from J. D. Billings, who owned over two hundred acres with frontage on Grand Traverse Bay. Known locally as Billings Heights, this southern section of the peninsula was relatively untouched, mostly wooded, and pristine. After purchasing the land, the Lathrops hired a local contractor, A. W. Wait, to build them a modest home with a view of West Grand Traverse Bay. They called their home *Edgewood.*

At the time, George and Cornelia resided in Jackson, Michigan, where George was successfully engaged in various business enterprises. The Lathrops had six children; although only three sons survived to adulthood: Arthur, George Jr., and William. In 1885, after George retired, he and Cornelia moved from Jackson to make Traverse City their permanent home. The Lathrops eventually purchased more than fifty acres on the peninsula, including the high bluff behind Edgewood, where George planted fruit trees and a garden that provided fresh food for their guests.

Above: George Lathrop (circa 1870)

Right: George Lathrop (1880)

A gathering of women at Edgewood. (1890)

Above: Cornelia Lathrop (circa 1870)

Left: Cornelia Lathrop (1895)

The Lathrops soon found that others enjoyed the beauty of Edgewood. Thus, out of a necessity to accommodate visiting friends and family, they decided an addition was needed. Less than a year later, they again hired Mr. Wait to build a second cottage just to the north of their home.

Above: The second cottage the Lathrops built at Edgewood. (1885)

Below: The road leading into Edgewood. (1897)

A few years later, at the urging of several friends, Mrs. Lathrop decided that she would open their home to paying summer boarders. One of the visitors that summer was Miss Lucy Lewis, also from Jackson, Michigan. She enjoyed the area so much that she purchased ten acres of land north of the Lathrop's home. In 1889, Miss Lewis built the first of three cottages.

Above: George and Cornelia Lathrop's grandson Philip. (circa 1900)
Below: Edgewood Resort (circa 1900)

Several other people bought land nearby and the community of Edgewood eventually grew to include ten cottages. Edgewood was never officially platted, but what became known as *Edgewood Resort* started about a mile from the Traverse City city limits along the eastern shore of West Grand Traverse Bay, continuing north and ending about a half mile past the Lathrop's home on McKinley Road. Defining the actual borders of Edgewood Resort is difficult because a two-mile stretch of Peninsula Drive was often referred to as "Edgewood." (See map adjacent to page 1.)

Unlike the Lathrops, most of the cottage owners lived elsewhere during the colder months of the year, and spent the summers at Edgewood or rented their homes to others when they were unoccupied. Many visitors came from Jackson, but others hailed from Detroit, Grand Rapids, and Chicago.

Edgewood differed from other popular resorts in the region, such as the well-promoted Omena Resort located across the bay in Leelanau County, because it was a "cottage resort" rather than a platted project. Unlike Omena Resort, which was built by developers with the purpose of attracting people to a well-planned community and lots were platted for cottages and hotels to accommodate many visitors, Edgewood grew cottage by cottage.

An article that appeared in the *Grand Traverse Herald* on March 17, 1892, compares other resorts in the area to the fast-growing Omena Resort:

> Comfortable hotels are already provided at all the towns on the bay and at Traverse Point, Neahtawanta, Traverse Beach, Fountain Point, with limited but homelike and exceedingly pleasant accommodations at Edgewood, while at Omena is the large hotel especially noticed in this article.

The large resorts took no business away from Edgewood. In June 1896, the *Grand Traverse Herald* reported:

> Beautiful Edgewood: While all the summer resorts are sending out prospectuses and advertising their hotels, Edgewood is turning tourists away. Every available nook and corner has been engaged until late in the fall, and the guests began coming in early May.

A selection of postcards from 1900–1905.

Later in the same year, another article reported that approximately seventy guests were at Edgewood at one time, and as late as mid-September there were still many tourists who were planning to stay well into October.

Although the Lathrops originally built Edgewood as a retirement home, it evolved into something much more.

THE EARLY YEARS

In the early years of the resort, Edgewood could accommodate about sixty people. Most of the cottages were used for sleeping only, while meals were prepared and served in the lower level of the Lathrop home. Mrs. Lathrop employed a cook and other servants, such as laundresses, positions for which she advertised in the local newspaper. Evidence of one local girl hired to work at Edgewood was found in the form of her name and a date written on a cottage wall.

Lucy Lewis, however, brought her own help. "Miss Lewis of Jackson has arrived at Edgewood for the summer . . . She brought with her a housekeeper and colored help, and her cottages will be filled this summer with tourists from Jackson."[1]

In addition to dining, visitors also gathered at the Lathrop's for entertainment. Mrs. Lathrop was an active member of the Traverse City Women's Club and hosted various social occasions. One event was held in the summer of 1894. Mrs. Lathrop and Miss Lewis co-hosted a party for a Traverse City businessman and his wife, Mr. and Mrs. J. W. Milliken. The previous year, Mr. Milliken had fashioned a "portable cottage" and taken it to the Chicago World's Fair. A reunion was held at Edgewood and about one hundred people attended. Dinner was served and local talent provided entertainment.

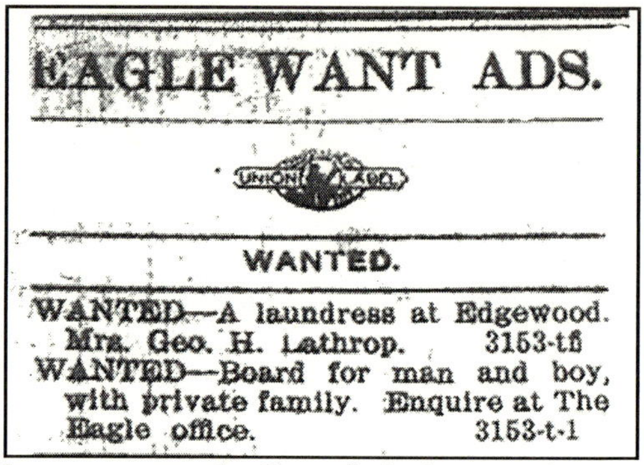

EAGLE WANT ADS.

WANTED.

WANTED—A laundress at Edgewood. Mrs. Geo. H. Lathrop. 3153-tf

WANTED—Board for man and boy, with private family. Enquire at The Eagle office. 3153-t-1

It was common for Cornelia Lathrop to place ads for needed help in the local papers.

Miss Lucy Lewis held numerous gatherings at her cottages as well. During the 1890s she was involved with the Shakespeare Club, a group of ladies that met once a week to read and discuss the works of William Shakespeare. She also organized the Tourists' Club (as she had in Jackson, too) and held most of the meetings at her Edgewood home. These meetings were informative gatherings where a guest speaker told of his or her travels to foreign countries.

Miss Lewis and the Lathrops were active members of the Congregational Church and hosted meetings of the Congregational Foreign Missionary Society and the Bridge Builders, a group that Miss Lewis founded. Many of these events were reported on in the newspaper, such as in the following that appeared in the *Traverse City Morning Record* on June 17, 1897:

> An afternoon at Edgewood: The Woman's Foreign Missionary Society of the Congregational Church and the Bridge Builders spent a pleasant time at Edgewood yesterday afternoon and early evening. There were 70 in the company some of whom went out on bicycles, some in carriages and others in omnibuses. The afternoon was devoted to a missionary meeting, the principal

Top: The Women's Club gathered regularly at Edgewood. Cornelia Lathrop is seated on the far left. (circa 1892)

Middle: A gathering of the Shakespeare Club. (1912)

Left: Dr. Maggie McKellar visited Edgewood to speak about her missionary work in India.

> feature of which was a very entertaining and instructive address by Dr. Maggie McKellar, returned missionary from India. Mrs. McKellar gave graphic and pleasing accounts of her work among the women of India and in the hospitals, and exhibited some photographs of scenes which she dilated upon in her talk. The address was intensely interesting and the engaging manner of Dr. McKellar made the recital additionally interesting. At 5 o'clock the ladies were joined by about a dozen gentlemen, honorary members of the missionary society when the entire company enjoyed a tempting spread supplied by Mrs. Lathrop. The early evening was devoted to visiting and informal missionary talks by Dr. McKellar. Later a number enjoyed sailing and rowing on the bay in the moonlight. This was one of the most pleasant gatherings ever held by the society and one of the many where the hospitality of the Lathrop cottage is made pleasantly manifest.

In 1898, the local bicycle club held a party at Edgewood. Following is a review of the event:

> One of the most enjoyable society events of the summer was the bicycle party and marshmallow roast given the young ladies of the O.B.C. and a number of gentlemen friends by the misses Gertrude Higgins and Gayle Griswold Thursday evening. The party met at the home of Miss Higgins and proceeded to Edgewood, where they had been invited by Miss Lewis. The dock and shaded grounds were gay with Japanese lanterns and four driftwood fires on the beach cast a ruddy glow on the glassy water, mingling with the tints of the sunset. Later the moon made a bright path across the bay, the whole making a picture long to be remembered. The evening passed all too swiftly in toasting marshmallows over the glowing coals, visiting and singing, and it was a late hour before the moon looked down upon the party as they rode merrily home.[2]

As it is today, the proximity to the bay was one of the main attractions of Edgewood. Although the shoreline was rocky, the Lathrops had two small docks and the water was fairly shallow. Guests could go sailing, rowing, and fishing. During the early years of the resort, small passenger boats were able to berth at the dock and transport guests to Traverse City. Eventually though, as water levels changed, the passenger boats were no longer able to access Edgewood's docks.

The high bluff behind the Lathrop's home was often a destination point; tourists enjoyed driving to the top to enjoy the panoramic view across the bay and to watch sunsets.

> The "Bridge builders" held their June rally at the pretty summer home of Miss Lucy Lewis, at Edgewood, Fri. evening. Over fifty were present and the evening was one long to be remembered. Soon after arriving, a picnic supper was served in one of Miss Lewis's cottages, which was beautifully decorated with daisies and ferns. After this part of the program had been carried out the party scattered, some going to the shore to enjoy the sunset, others climbing the high bluff at the rear of the cottages, while a number gathered at one of the cottages to enjoy the mandolin playing of Richard Ewing, of Grand Rapids, a member of the U. of M. banjo club. It was far into the evening before the party returned to their homes in the city.[3]

Boat excursions around the bay were common. Visitors traveled to other resorts, such as Omena, Leelanau Hotel, and the Park Place Hotel in Traverse City, to sightsee and visit with the guests of those hotels. As reported in the *Traverse City Morning Record* on August 8, 1898:

> One of the most delightful social events of the summer season was given at Park Place last night. The spacious parlors of the hotel were thronged with local society people, resorters from Traverse Beach and Edgewood, and the guests of the hotel. . . . the guests enjoying alternately the social amusements provided.

Resort visitors picnicked on Marion Island, where the small bay steamers could dock. These excursions were often noted in the local paper. A July 25, 1905, clipping from the *Traverse City Evening Record* reported that "Mr. B. and family of Jackson and Mrs. Bacon of Grand Rapids, who are rusticating at Edgewood this summer, are taking in the beautiful bay trip to Northport and return today on the steamer *Columbia*."

Top: The steamer Columbia transported visitors to and from Edgewood.

Middle: Philip Lathrop canoeing with two female friends.

Bottom: Excursions to Marion Island were frequent.

Above: A postcard from 1905.

Left: Philip Lathrop, George and Cornelia's grandson. (circa 1910)

Below: Grandma Cornelia Lathrop. (circa 1900)

Another boat, the *Chequamegon*, also plied the bay and took tourists out to enjoy the beauty of the region. In the June 17, 1907, edition of the *Traverse City Evening Record* it was reported that

> . . . 200 more [people] accompanied by Horst's orchestra, went around the island. The warm offshore wind, the moonlight and the slight swell on the bay, made the trip as enjoyable as possible.

Marshmallow roasts over bonfires on the beach were a popular pastime, especially with the younger guests.

Other entertainment came from the guests themselves, as many played instruments or sang. Newspaper articles mention some of these activities: "There are two very fine machines, a Victor and a Victrola, at present at Edgewood, and the guests have been enjoying oratorios and operas to their hearts' content. Among the guests there are one or two very fine pianists so the music lovers have been feasting accordingly."[4] "… chairs were arranged in a semi-circle in the grove in front of Miss Lewis's … the piano was brought to the door and a delightful program listened to by all … never has a concert been more enjoyed than that which was given with a piazza for a stage and all outdoors for an audience room."[5] "Miss Lucy Lewis opened her cottage to the young ladies for an ice cream social."[6] "Gilbert Wilson of Traverse City brought his telescope out to Edgewood on Wednesday and the evening was spent on the dock where Jupiter and Venus entertained the guests."[7] "The dining room at Edgewood was given over to the guests on Tuesday evening, and some very clever charades were given."[8] "Miss Marie Knibloe, a very talented dramatic reader, impersonator, vocalist and whistler, gave a program last night at Edgewood that was much enjoyed by the tourists . . . the program included several comedy selections, vocal and whistling numbers . . . a literary and musical treat of the highest order of excellence."[9] "The ladies were requested to bring their thimbles . . . prizes were awarded for the daintiest sewing."[10] "The Edgewood Reading Club met at Mrs. Minty's cottage last Saturday afternoon and read and discussed a book of short stories by VanDyke."[11]

On August 8, 1895, Mrs. Martha Bates wrote an article about

Edgewood that appeared in the *Grand Traverse Herald.* Following is an excerpt:

> The beautiful woods have been carefully preserved; and the delightful rustic seats among the trees on the shore find frequent visitors, while the winding paths up the hillside and down the shore ring with the merry laughter of the children at their play . . . This year two old boats drawn up on the shore are filled with beautiful flowers, making a pretty bit of color against the background of bay and woods. One of the favorite amusements of the guests is driving, fine roads extending to Ne-ah-ta-wanta and Old Mission on the north and to the city, two and one half miles away, and from there in all directions on the south. A road has been opened up this year from Billings Heights along the top of the high bluff just back of Edgewood to a crossroad beyond, giving a bit of woodland and a beautiful view of the bay the rest of the way. The high, steep bluff, heavily wooded with primeval forest, comes down to a level terrace . . . with winding paths through slender birches and under the great pines, in which the wind sings always a low refrain to the rhythm of the splashing waters on the yellow sands below.
>
> A peculiarity of Edgewood is the delightful class of people who make this their home for the summer. Among the guests have been judges, eminent divines, college presidents and professors, doctors, lawyers, high state officials and missionaries, with their families, and rare treats in the way of talks by many famous people have been given under the trees or in the capacious parlors. Mr. Lathrop has a fine fruit and vegetable farm on the hills back of the resort as the boarders have good reason to know. Although many come and go at Edgewood during the summer, the general number remains the same, as the vacancies are filled almost as soon as they occur.

Due to Mrs. Lathrop's skills as a hostess, Edgewood continued to be a favorite resort throughout the 1890s and into the first decade of the twentieth century. In August 1890, an article in the *Grand Traverse Herald* sang her praises:

> The Lathrop cottages and two of the Lewis cottages, forming what may perhaps be termed Edgewood proper, are in a measure under one management, having a general dining room in the cottage occupied as a residence by Mr. and Mrs. Lathrop. All together, however, they form a delightful home, over which Mrs. Lathrop presides as its good genius, and devotes herself to the comfort and pleasure of her guests in a very charming and exceedingly successful manner. No one comes here for a visit, be it of longer or shorter duration, who does not come again if it be possible to do so.

Mrs. Lathrop was known in the community as a generous, kindhearted woman who took an active role in charities, the Women's Club, Ladies Library Association, and her church organizations.

"AT EDGEWOOD – Mrs. John McIntosh entertained the ladies Whist club at her cottage at Edgewood yesterday afternoon, where whist was engaged in to while away the afternoon hours. In the evening the gentlemen were expected to take part in the fish supper where covers were laid for 24 guests. In the evening a bon fire was built on the beach and marshmallows roasted and all enjoyed a pleasant evening. The gentlemen became so enthusiastic in building the bon fire that they builded better than they knew, for the fire was seen at the docks and some launches put off for Edgewood to see whose cottage was burning, but it was only the bon fire of the Whist club."

Traverse City Evening Record, July 28, 1909 (Whist was the forerunner of the card game bridge and, yes, "builded" is the word used in the article.)

THE LATHROPS

George and Cornelia Lathrop opened their home to two young girls, both of whom were orphaned in childhood. Ten-year-old Sophia Morrison is listed in the 1880 census as an adopted daughter. Sophia's parents died in New York City when she was a toddler. Sophia grew up with the Lathrops in Jackson and was always loved as one of the family.

In April 1889, Sophia married William O. Holden, a young man from Traverse City. Sophia, who had observed her adoptive mother's skills, also became a well-loved hostess and helped William at the two hotels he managed—the Park Place Hotel in Traverse City and the Roaring Brook Inn in Harbor Springs.

On the 22d of April, 1889, Mr. Holden was united in marriage to Miss Sophia Morrison, who was born in New York city, on the 3d of September, 1869. Her parents died when she was a child, and she was reared in the home of George H. Lathrop, of Jackson, Michigan. Mr. and Mrs. Holden have one child, Margaret, who was born on the 29th of April, 1890, and who is now attending the public schools.

Top: Margaret Menauch. (circa 1905)

Middle and bottom: Postcards from Edgewood Resort. (circa 1905)

In early 1892, George and Cornelia took in Margaret Menauch as a foster child. Margaret and her siblings were orphaned when their father was killed in a quarry accident in Detroit. The children were sent to different places, but possibly through a connection with the Masonic Lodge, of which Margaret's father and George were both members, Margaret was welcomed into the Lathrop home. The Lathrops loved Margaret as their own daughter and she remained at Edgewood for four years, until her marriage to William Wilson, the son of a prominent local farmer, in 1896. After her marriage, Margaret and her husband lived only a few miles from Edgewood.

In a 1994 interview, Jim Wilson, their son, who was then eighty-eight years old, remembered this about Margaret's connection to Edgewood:

> She and her sister and brother came to Michigan as foster children. Her father was a stone mason who worked in a quarry. He was killed . . . they came up to Beechwood [*sic* meaning Edgewood] and they had all of these cottages. . . . That's where my dad met my mother for she was a foster child in there. . . . She remembered the President of the University of Michigan who would come up to Edgewood every summer. He stayed there and she remembers they had a word game they would play. They were given a word and they would have to spell it and then give the definition of it. You could never stump her on hardly any word. She was a smart lady.[12]

~ • ~

On May 21, 1900, after a short illness, at the age of seventy-five, Mr. George Howland Lathrop died at Edgewood. His remains were taken to their old home in Jackson for interment. A beautifully written obituary was printed in the *Traverse City Morning Record*, a portion of which gives the following description of Edgewood and George H. Lathrop:

> In 1885 Mr. and Mrs. Lathrop moved to Traverse City, making their home at the pretty spot there in all its primitive wilderness, on the bay shore, since widely known as Edgewood.

> It was a dear home, beautiful for location and beautiful within the sweet spirit of love that goes to the making of all nice homes. Friends came to visit them and begged to stay, and leaving, begged to come again. The house overflowed with delighted visitors, pretty cottages were built for more ample accommodations, and the home Edgewood became Edgewood the Beautiful Summer Resort, whose name is known and loved throughout the state and beyond. It was not a mere boarding place; it was a delightful home to which those who came once came again, as birds come north for their summer nesting, and always bringing others with them, and it has always been a place of which Traverse City has been proud.
>
> Mr. Lathrop was a Christian gentleman. His children and grandchildren can say what is rare praise, that they have never heard an unkind word from him.

Mrs. Lathrop continued to run the resort that year, with the help of her sister Sarah Turner and friend Hattie Bacon, who was a regular guest.

GUESTS

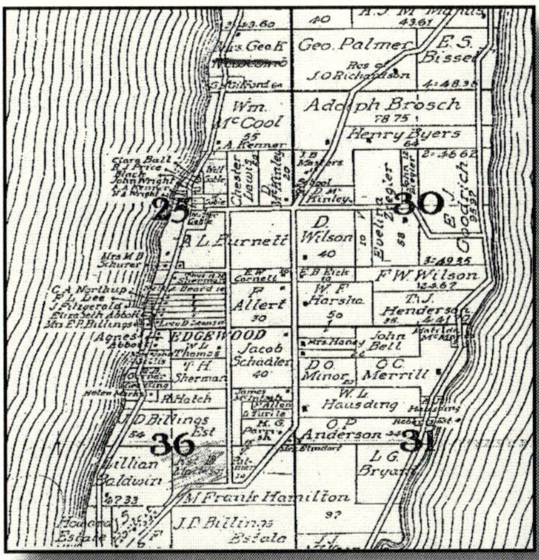

As wonderful as life was at Edgewood, it was not without tragedy. Mr. James B. Angell, President of the University of Michigan, and his wife, spent the summer of 1895 at Edgewood. The following summer, their son Alexis brought his family to Edgewood. On July 14, 1896, Alexis's son Tom, who was about eleven years old, went swimming by himself. After Tom was not seen for a while, a group went looking for him. They found his body near the dock. Family legend says Tom jumped off the dock into shallow water and broke his neck, although his obituary says he drowned. The Angell family never returned to Edgewood after this horrible tragedy.

Accidents were rare at Edgewood, and many people returned year after year. The family of Detroit neurologist Dr. Charles Hitchcock

†EDGEWOOD, MICH.

Lathrop Cottage	Mrs. G. H. Lathrop	25	1.00	5.00 to 7.00
Gray Stone Cottage	Mrs. M. B. Schryer		On application	
Two Cottages	Miss Lewis		On application	

"EDGEWOOD"

Delightful Summer Resort on Grand Traverse Bay. Famed throughout the country for its excellent management and fine accommodations.

MRS. GEO. H. LATHROP

Top: 1908 Michigan Resort brochure listing.

Second from top: 1905 Peninsula Township brochure listing.

Middle right: Alexis Angell with his wife and two children.

Middle left: Dr. Joseph B. Griswold. (circa 1912)

Bottom: Dr. Charles Hitchcock. (circa 1918)

spent several summers at Edgewood. The George Smalley family of Jackson, Michigan, relatives of Miss Lewis, returned to the resort several times, as well as members of the Penney family from Detroit and the Williamson and Coit families of Grand Rapids. An article that appeared in the *Traverse City Evening Record* on June 29, 1911 stated that "Mrs. Penney has been a visitor at Edgewood for more than twenty years." Mrs. Hattie J. (Griswold) Bacon spent every summer at the resort from 1889 until her death in 1916. And her brother, Dr. Joseph Griswold, and his family also spent many summers at Edgewood. An article in the June 17, 1912, issue of the *Traverse City Record-Eagle* mentions Mrs. Georgiene Torrey of Jackson, Michigan, as returning to the resort for the fifteenth consecutive year.

The homelike atmosphere, where children were warmly welcomed, made these families want to return. Many of the regular visitors were either related or knew each other from their home cities. As was common then, many families arrived at the resort together, with the wives and children staying for an extended time, while the husbands returned to their homes and jobs during the week. Several prominent people visited Edgewood, including Michigan Supreme Court Judge Edward Cahill, Professor Hugh Scott of the Chicago Theological Seminary, and Bishop Edward R. Atwell of the Episcopal Church in Kansas.

After the turn of the twentieth century, several more people invested in Edgewood land. Between 1902 and 1912 another building "boom" occurred with the following people erecting cottages within a half mile of the Lathrop cottage: Fred Lee of Chicago, Miss Agnes Abbott, Charles Dye of Traverse City, Mrs. Harry VanderVoort of Chicago, Mrs. Mary B. Schryer of Traverse City, and Martin Tanner of Saginaw.

TRUNKS! TRUNKS! TRUNKS! COMING IN A STREAM FROM RESORTS, TELL STORY OF A VANISHING SUMMER

It's "Trunks! Trunks! Trunks" as Kipling might chant were he writing of trivial things nowadays. Every day they are coming in from surrounding resorts loaded high upon the drays and motor trucks, all headed for the steamer dock or the railway stations, and they tell the story of the end of the summer. Locked up within their scored strapped sides are the secrets of many lives, the keepsakes of a summer, the wrecks of blasted loves and tokens of high hopes, jumbling and jangling and mixing together in common association, and democracy, amid frilly things and bathing suits.

There are steamer trunks and the kind we used to call saratogas; there are boxes and chests and packing cases, class and super-class, all piled on the same wagons because the rush for home is on and baggage men are not respectors of caste. The clerk's cash is as good as that of the idle rich to the man who drives the trunk wagon.

And where they have been these varied containers of clothing and mementos? It is interesting to consider that and conjecture. There's a new one here and there, which may have been purchased just for the little vacation in the northland. On top reposes a steamer trunk which looks as though it has traveled over the sands of Arabia's deserts and perhaps it has. There's another which bears the stickers of the Hotel Cecil in London, and half a dozen continental pensions and hotels. Perhaps it is an imposter like its owner. Perhaps it has never been farther into foreign lands than Windsor, Canada. There's another, with stout round corners, and film edges, which bears few marks, but which looks like an officer's trunk. Maybe his widow is using it this summer.

But anyway, it's "Trunks! Trunks! Trunks!" And the stream of them tell the story of many things, if one could but peep into them. Right now they are going home to the four corners of the compass, some to hope, some to pleasure and some to drudgery. They tell the story of the end of the summer, the greatest summer, the greatest season the Grand Traverse Region has had in many a year.

Traverse City Record-Eagle
September 4, 1919 (author unknown)

THE LATER YEARS

ONE of many promotional pamphlets published around 1908 listed the capacity and prices of hundreds of hotels and boarding houses from Traverse City to Mackinac Island. The main lodge at Edgewood is included, as well as Mrs. Schryer's cottage *Graystone*, and Miss Lewis's cottages. The cost to stay at the Lathrop cottage was one dollar a day or five to seven dollars for a week, with a capacity for twenty-five people.

By 1908, Mrs. Lathrop was having difficulty running the dining hall herself. She was nearly eighty years old and the work had become too much for her. In May 1909, Mrs. Lathrop asked the Traverse City Board of Trade to help her find someone to run the dining room. Mrs. Nannie Bennett took the job. Mrs. Bennett was the daughter of Civil War Cavalry General R. H. G. Minty and

Grace Abbott, who was the sister of Agnes, Elizabeth, and Charles Abbott, who all owned Edgewood cottages.

Edgewood continued to be popular and a steady flow of resorters filled the cottages. The July 25, 1911, issue of the *Traverse City Evening Record* states: "Edgewood is full to overflowing, its small dining room was taxed to the utmost on Sunday last and applications for rooms have been refused for some time." Three days later, it was reported: "Edgewood is losing some guests today who are obliged to leave because the rooms they occupy are engaged for the remainder of the season by others who arrive tonight, and there are no more accommodations to be had."

The Pere Marquette Railroad published a booklet for the 1912 tourist season that described the summer resorts in Northern Michigan. Mrs. George S. (Nannie) Bennett is listed as running "The Lismore at Edgewood Cottage Resort—with new central dining hall building, having nine guest rooms; accommodates eighty in dining room . . ." The Lismore was to be a new dining hall across the road from the cottage Mrs. Bennett purchased in 1909. It was located a few cottages to the north of the Lathrop house.

According to several small articles in the paper, fish dinners were the main item on the menu. On June 13, 1910, the *Traverse City Record-Eagle* reported:

> Mrs. Bennett has charge of the dining room in the Edgewood hotel this season and the regular Thursday evening supper will be served, consisting of planked whitefish.

PLANKED FISH (*The Settlement Cook-Book*, 1903)

Fish is planked when baked on a board (hickory, oak or ash) in the oven. Place the board in oven until very hot. Place the fish on board, season with salt and pepper and a little butter, or split it and place it skin down on the board; brush with butter and dust with salt and pepper. Baste often with melted butter, and bake until a golden brown. Serve with parsley, lemon or pickles sliced. Whitefish is best served in this style.

Will Lathrop. (circa 1900)

Lillian Lathrop. (circa 1900)

Edgewood Cottage Resort—Address Miss Lucy D. Lewis; furnished cottages for rent for the season; excellent dining hall. For terms address Miss Lucy D. Lewis, 1003 Main Street West, Jackson, Mich., until June 1st; after that, Edgewood, via Traverse City. For information other than that of rental of cottages, address Mrs. Geo. S. Bennett, Traverse City, Edgewood rural delivery.

The Lismore, at Edgewood—Cottage resort with new central dining hall building, having nine guest rooms; accommodates eighty in dining room; rates on application. Cottages for rent. Until May 1st inquire of Mrs. Geo. S. Bennett, 422 South St., Traverse City; after May 1st, The Lismore, Edgewood, Traverse City.

Front: Arthur, mother Cornelia, her sister Sarah Turner, Lester Osborne, Alice Osborne Lathrop
Beck: Katherine, Jack, Lita, Ellery Preston, Florence, Harriet Seated:- Cornelia Preston

Photograph of Nannie Minty Bennett, the first child of R.H.G. and Grace, holding her own daughter Charlotte, dated Sept. 3rd 1903. [Judith Minty]

Top left: George Jr.

Top right: Helen Lathrop at Edgewood.

Middle left: Nannie Bennett and her daughter Charlotte. (1903)

Middle right: Harriet Lathrop.

Bottom: Edgewood Resort. (circa 1930)

Not only did the resort's guests use the dining facility, but Traverse City residents also enjoyed the good food. "Mrs. Bennett has her arrangements completed for opening the dining room at Edgewood on June 15. The fish suppers will be continued during the season as last year. Parties from the city who desire to take Sunday dinner at Edgewood should notify Mrs. Bennett the day before."[13]

Sadly, Mrs. Bennett died suddenly in February 1912,[14] and the new dining hall was never finished. To provide for the summer guests of 1912, Mary Kinnucan was hired as head of the Lathrop dining hall.

The June 17, 1912 *Traverse City Record-Eagle* informed readers that "Mrs. F.J. Kinnucan has taken the dining hall and is giving the best of service. Many of the Traverse City people are taking advantage of her good meals and autoing [sic] out there to partake of them."

Nineteen twelve was a year of drastic change at Edgewood. Not only did the resort lose Mrs. Bennett in February, but on July 9 Cornelia Lathrop died at her home at the age of eighty-two. During her life, Edgewood was a hub of social activity, but after Cornelia's death, Edgewood was never the same. For nearly thirty years Edgewood was well-known for society gatherings. Mrs. Lathrop's special skill as a hostess was sorely missed.

Only three months after Mrs. Lathrop's death, during Labor Day weekend, a series of storms hit the Grand Traverse region. Nearly four inches of rain fell over a three-day period. In the early morning hours of September 5, 1912, after being saturated with rain, the huge bluff behind the Lathrop home gave out. An article in the September 5, 1912 *Traverse City Record-Eagle* stated:

> **BURIED IN SAND: Lathrop Cottage and Dining Hall Damaged by Storm**
>
> Considerable damage was experienced on various parts of the peninsula during the recent storms, but it seems that the greatest havoc was wrought at Edgewood, when the big hill back of the dining room literally broke and came upon the big house full force. The kitchen stove was buried in three feet of sand and mud,

In a 1974 letter to her cousin Barbara Abbott, Charlotte wrote about her mother's death: "I was permitted to leave school early to go with mother. I think your father drove us to the R.R. station in Traverse City. It was snowing and the train was late. Mother agreed I might stay with her and return home alone after her train left. While we waited she printed and taught me to spell my middle name. We had a bag of horehound candy. The train finally came. She went to Detroit for surgery and two weeks later your mother took Grandmother [Grace Abbott Minty] and me to Detroit, but mother had died while we were on the train. I have never been back to Traverse City or Edgewood, but all through the years, particularly when I was in tropical countries I thought of the pine woods, the smell and the softness of pine needle paths from cottage to cottage."

For a year after her mother passed away, Charlotte Bennett Blair lived with an aunt. She was then sent to a school for girls in Staunton, Virginia. In late 1918, at the age of fifteen, she was taken in by her older brother George S. Bennett, Jr. who lived in Costa Rica and worked for a U.S.-run fruit company. She remained there, marrying a much older man, Henry Stirling Blair, on October 16, 1920. They had one son, Henry S. Blair Jr. Not much is known about how long she stayed in Central America. She and her husband moved to New Jersey, where he died, and by the 1970s she had settled in Niles, Michigan, where she lived until her death in 1985.

> while water stood in regular little ponds in all parts of the house. When Mrs. Kinnucan got out of bed she found herself standing in water nearly a foot deep. Other cottages were damaged to some extent, but nothing as compared with "Edgewood," the cottage built by the late Mrs. Lathrop, and from which the resort took its name.

Luckily the portion of the home that was destroyed was not where the guests and manager were sleeping. The northernmost part of the house that was heavily damaged was demolished and the home was renovated, although reduced in size. Edgewood reopened to serve the public and tourists the following spring.

After her death, Mrs. Lathrop's three surviving sons inherited the Edgewood property. They sold it in 1919. Even though the Lathrops no longer owned the cottages, members of their extended family continued to vacation at Edgewood through the 1920s and beyond. George and Cornelia's granddaughter Harriet brought her children to Traverse City, most likely renting one of the Edgewood cottages.

In the 1920s, the Lathrop property was parceled off. The 1912 washout had revealed a rich vein of gravel; Frank Wysong purchased the upper part of the property to use for a gravel and concrete business. Mr. Wysong had already established a company in the Traverse City area; the Edgewood property became his main source of gravel from the 1920s until the business closed.

As early as 1914, gravel was being extracted from the "Lathrop Pit," as it was called, for improvements on an east bay road. An article in the May 26, 1914 *Traverse City Record-Eagle* explained:

> . . . it is estimated that each team will make at least four round trips a day, and with fifty teams on the job . . .

With the idea of preserving the beauty of the Edgewood area, the Lathrops had the foresight to place a stipulation in the deed that only a certain section of the property could be used to open a gravel pit. The Wysongs agreed to "preserve the present contour of the land . . . shall not remove or destroy the said hill and the timber growing thereon on the land owned by them . . ." The Wysong Gravel Company was in business until about the mid-1980s.

Even without the Lathrops, Edgewood continued to be a popular resort destination. This article in the April 21, 1914 *Traverse City Record-Eagle*, seems to be reassuring readers that Edgewood would continue on.

> The Edgewood house has been thoroughly renovated and put in shape for the season . . . Mrs. F.J. Kinnucan has leased the Bennett cottage at Edgewood and will have entire control of the dining room and two cottages for the summer. There are a number of cottagers who are coming north much earlier than usual and Mrs. Kinnucan taking care of the dining room will enable all the resorters to come and remain as long as they wish. Edgewood is one of the popular resorts and the number of summer visitors has increased each year. Inquiries already received indicate that the number will be fully as large as in previous years.

Visitors came after Mrs. Lathrop's death, but unfortunately the years following the Lathrop era at Edgewood are not well-documented. Newspapers from May 1915 until January 1917 are not existent (at least this author could not locate any). It is doubtful that people traveled much in those years, with World War I foremost in the news and the local economy suffering. Plus the constant traffic of trucks to and from the gravel pit may have made the area less desirable to visitors.

Although the dining hall was closed when the family sold the property, the resort was not completely shut down. Starting in 1920, articles began to appear in the newspaper, with the opening of the Edgewood Inn, run by Traverse City residents John and Pearl Nelson. (See their story on page 56.) Also in 1920, a group of longtime cottage owners formed an association called "The Edgewood Improvement Society." The resort had suffered a decline for several years and the "object of the association [was] to be the promotion of whatever may be for the best interests and general good of this beautiful resort suburb . . ."[15] The members of the group were Frank James, Mr. and Mrs. Wallace Keep, Emily Billings, Frank Somers, and Martin W. Tanner. Mr. Somers had encountered a group similar to this one in Colorado and hoped it might help revive the resort.

A LOOK AT LOCAL INDUSTRY

WYSONG GRAVEL COMPANY

A three-day rain in 1918 washed out the main lodge and dining hall at Edgewood, an early resort development on West Bay, two miles north of Traverse City on the peninsula.

But the waters that pushed this famous resort structure into the bay also revealed a rich vein of gravel in the hill back of the resort—and thus was born what is now known as the Wysong Gravel Company, 6972 Peninsula.

Since purchase of the gravel bank from Carl Bye in 1923, over two million yards of sand and gravel have been excavated as the enterprise participated in the growth and development of the region. For example, materials from the Wysong pit were used in construction of the Park Place Hotel and the Boardman River Dam in the early 1930's.

But the history of the Wysong gravel business goes beyond 1923. L. F. Wysong purchased the gravel pit and cement block factory operated by Frank Goodrich on W. Front street at Madison in 1910. The enterprise was then known as L. F. Wysong and Sons, since Charles, Frank, and Ben, sons of the senior Wysong, were also in the business.

The gravel pit in those days extended south along Madison to Sixth street. A hill in this area was completely removed.

On April 29, 1919, while the sons were serving in World War I, a half interest in the business was sold to Charles Jeffries, a local potato buyer. This partnership continued until the death of Mr. Jeffries in 1922. The following year, Mr. Wysong purchased the Jeffries interest.

From 1910 to 1923, the business converted from hand power and horses to modern machinery and dump trucks. Wysong was the first in this region to use dump trucks.

When the property on the peninsula was taken over, the Wysongs moved into one of the remaining frame cottages at the site. The structure was modernized with a stone veneer on the outside and remodeling in the interior. Many famous names of resorters of the past were found on the registrations, including John Gilbert and Ruth Bryan Owen.

A by-product of the Wysong operation on the peninsula has been the creation of a sand beach over a two-mile stretch along the shore. Sand which came from the lake bed during the glacier period has been sluiced back into the bay as a result of the washing of gravel, and the sand has then been redeposited by lake action to cover what was once stony beach.

Officers of the business now are Earl Wysong, president; Ruth Wysong, his sister, secretary; and Jon Manson, treasurer. The enterprise was incorporated as Wysong Gravel Company in 1955 with Frank Wysong, one of the brothers, as vice-president. He has since retired.

The payroll today averages about $24,000 annually, and employment fluctuates between four and 10 persons. Purchases of local goods and services come to about $25,000 yearly.

Summer residents and others enjoy driving through the pit to the highest plateau for a breathtaking view of the bay and the hills to the west. They find Petoskey stones aplenty, and sometimes a tiny diamond is discovered glistening in the gravel. Small nuggets of gold are also occasionally picked out in the washing operation, but none of these rare finds compares with the value of the sand and gravel that the rains of 44 years ago brought to light. And it is estimated that the pit will last another 40 years, as the 23-acre hill is still less than half excavated.

This informational series is brought to you in the hopes that you will share our strong convictions that we should all — SUPPORT LOCAL INDUSTRIES!

Oleson's Food Stores of Traverse City

Article printed in the *Traverse City Record-Eagle* on November 24, 1962.

Nineteen twenty must have been the best year for the resort in a long time. "Not for many years has Edgewood had so many visitors or taken on so much life as during this closing season, and much good can be accomplished by a united and neighborly spirit fostered by just such an organization as has now come into life in this summer resort."[16]

The opening of the new Edgewood Inn was a definite asset, bringing in more visitors. Frank James and Wallace Keep each owned several of the Edgewood cottages, which they purchased after the original owners had passed away. They attempted to bring Edgewood back, but it never was the same as it had been during the heyday of the 1890s and early 1900s.

By 1930, Edgewood was a private residence used only during the summer. Over the years it would be owned by several families. When the current owners purchased the house in the early 1970s, it consisted of one large room that was used as the dining hall, a small kitchen, and the upstairs was an open, dormitory-style sleeping area. With the renovations made over the last thirty years, the home now has very little resemblance to the way it looked when the Lathrops owned it.

The Donnely home.
Top: circa 1970
Middle: 2006
Bottom: 2006

THE COTTAGES AT EDGEWOOD

BITTERSWEET COTTAGE

According to a longtime resident of the area, this house was transported across the frozen bay from Greilickville to Edgewood by being placed on sleds and pulled by horses. The exact year this occurred is unknown, but most likely it happened in the mid-1890s. The building was placed on a tall foundation on the shore, across the road from the Lathrop home. It was added by the Lathrops to provide additional accommodations for the ever-growing number of visitors each year.

It was called "Bittersweet Cottage" because of the large number of bittersweet vines that grew along the shore near the house.[17] For many years, it was the only building on the bayside of the road. It is featured in several vintage photographs of Edgewood.

In 1934, Mr. and Mrs. William Wiesler purchased the cottage and

winterized it a few years later for year-round living. Their daughter Rhea recalled that even in the 1930s and early 1940s, their summer home seemed very isolated. There was only one other home on the waterside of the road between the intersection of Peninsula Drive and Center Road (about one and a half miles away) at the city limits for many years. A nice sandy beach covered the shore; this was a result of the Wysong's gravel production on the hill behind the other cottages. Bittersweet Cottage is no longer standing.

> A by-product of the Wysong operation on the peninsula has been the creation of a sand beach over a two-mile stretch along the shore. Sand . . . has been sluiced back into the bay as a result of the washing of gravel, and the sand has been re-deposited by lake action to cover what was once stony beach.[18]

Top: Rhea Wiesler (l) and friends at Bittersweet Cottage. (circa 1939)

Middle: Bittersweet Cottage. (circa 1939)

Bottom: Rhea Wiesler (r) and friend on beach at Bittersweet Cottage. (circa 1940)

BIRCHWOOD, HEPATICA, AND ARBUTUS COTTAGES

Miss Lucy Lewis owned ten acres just to the north of the Lathrop's property. In 1889, she built Birchwood Cottage (the name was later changed to Trillium.) The following year, she had two more cottages built by contractor Lewis L. Ensign—a five-room cottage named Hepatica Cottage and a seven-room cottage called Arbutus Cottage. These homes cost Miss Lewis between $500 and $700 each to build.

In 1894, phone service was connected to Trillium Cottage. The *Herald* reported that "Miss Lewis' cottage "Trillium Lodge," at Edgewood, has been connected with the city telephone exchange—No.15, four rings."[19] For many years, hers was the only home at Edgewood with a telephone.

Miss Lewis owned the cottages until she died at the age of eighty, in January 1918. The ten acres and three cottages were sold to Wallace and Iva Keep in 1919. The Keeps were from Saginaw, Michigan, and had been visitors to Edgewood as early as 1910. They continued to rent out the cottages to summertime guests. They also owned other Edgewood cottages; one to the north of Edgewood which had originally been built for Judge Roscoe Corbett in 1898.

In 1936, the Keeps sold the three Lewis cottages to newlyweds James G. and Alice Thirlby. The Thirlbys added a kitchen, indoor plumbing, and modernized the rustic cottage with upgraded electrical wiring and beautiful pine paneling throughout before they moved in. The Thirlbys raised four children there, enjoying the beauty of Edgewood just as the people who stayed there before them. Photographs taken in the 1930s show that the three cottages changed little from when they were built forty years before.

The Thirlbys eventually sold two of the cottages, maintaining one as their residence until 2005, when they sold it.

As of 2011, the three buildings Miss Lucy Lewis had built are still standing; the middle one is used as a summer home while the southernmost house has also undergone major renovations over the years.

In an interview with Mrs. Alice Thirlby in January 2003, she was asked about her memories of the area in the 1930s. She spoke

Above: The Thirlby cottage. (circa 1937)

Left: The Southern Cottage. (circa 1940)

Above right: The Southern Cottage. (circa 2005)

Above left: The Lovett Cottage. (circa 2005)

Bottom left: The middle Thirlby cottage. (circa 1940)

of trees quite close to the edges of the rounded gravel road, which was difficult to drive on. This stretch of road has a history of close calls and bad accidents.[20]

As early as 1906, the Edgewood residents expressed their concerns about the speed of automobiles in the area and the safety of their children. Several of the regular residents had their complaints published in the newspaper. Again in 1910 and 1911, the Edgewood residents complained about speeding cars. Twenty years later, in 1931, after many complaints from Edgewood visitors and residents, the highway department placed a restricted speed zone through the winding, narrow stretch near Edgewood. Over the years, the road has been adjusted by the county to remove some of its curves. In 2011, homes line both sides of the road and it is a main thoroughfare up the west shore of the peninsula. Although the 35-mph speed limit is still in effect, some residents continue to be concerned about the traffic. Below are excerpts from various newspapers.

This stretch of road near Edgewood has been the scene of numerous fatal accidents.

Traverse City Evening Record, May 22, 1906
Reckless Autoists at Edgewood
The residents of Edgewood have been much annoyed of late, especially on Sundays by speeders who seem to forget that there are many small children in the cottages close to the road. Owing to the woods, children may easily be run over and crippled or killed outright by the heavy machines. The undersigned residents of Edgewood are asking themselves whether it is going to require an accident of this kind to bring these reckless speeders to a due regard for the law and for the right of pedestrians and cyclists to use the drive in safety.

Mrs. Geo. H. Lathrop, Mrs. H. G. Bacon, L.D. Lewis,
Harriet D. Newcomb, C.J. Abbott, D.A. Burnett, F.L Lee,
T.A. Jenkins, Robert J. Price.

Grand Traverse Herald, July 7, 1908
Edgewood residents had a complaint to make. Last year, they had signs up asking the auto drivers to come slow through the resort because of the number of children. This year, they found the signs removed and the machines come through the winding wooded road at a high rate of speed making it dangerous.

Traverse City Evening Record, June 21, 1910
Complaint comes from Edgewood that the auto drivers again this year are driving too fast through the resort and that they even do not sound a warning. As there are a number of children there who must cross the road to get to the bay, there is always the chance of a serious accident.

Traverse City Record-Eagle, June 13, 1911
The residents at Edgewood are protesting against the rate of speed at which automobiles pass through the resort. As there are many small children there who find it necessary to cross the road, there is liable to be a serious accident unless the drivers cut down their pace when out on their pleasure expeditions.

Traverse City Record-Eagle, July 1931
A second restricted speed zone has been established on the Peninsula in the Edgewood territory where the narrow, winding shore drive has brought complaints from summer residents.

ABBOTT COTTAGES

The two cottages to the north of the Lewis homes were built in 1889. Miss Elizabeth Abbott of Grand Rapids purchased one cottage in October 1890 and owned it until a few years before her death in 1925. Elizabeth's sister Agnes owned a cottage at Edgewood called "Southfield." It was built around 1904 and was located just to the south of the Lathrop property. Agnes did not spend as much time at Edgewood as Elizabeth did as Agnes often traveled abroad to visit relatives in England.

Elizabeth's and Agnes's great niece Charlotte (the daughter of Nannie Minty-Bennett, who ran the Edgewood dining hall for several years) described her aunts in a letter many years later:

> Agnes Abbott was a slight, gentle, dainty woman whose cottage in Edgewood I loved to visit. She had a colorful garden surrounded by a low white picket fence. There was a special corner where she helped me bury dead birds and small animals found by me as I wandered through the nearby pine woods. She had lovely antique furniture, and a tea set of fine white china with sky-blue dots around the edge. Cambric tea was particularly delicious in those cups. The cottage was white and green, open and airy. The floors were covered with Japanese matting, giving the cottage a lovely special fragrance.
>
> Elizabeth, Aunt Bess, was dark and sturdy and very precise. She taught me to knit. She insisted upon the proper use of my finger to throw the yarn even though my hands were too small to reach. Even today I feel I must finish a row before putting down my knitting. Her house was a mustardy yellow. It always seemed shut

> up against the sun. Every table, chair and shelf was neatly stacked with books, magazines and papers. At the age of six to eight, as I was when I remember these two maiden ladies, my great aunts, they appeared to be totally different. Each lived in her cottage from early spring until late fall when they closed the cottages and took off for trips, at least I remember stories of the Swiss Alps and the Scottish moors.
>
> I loved Aunt Agnes and was delightfully afraid of Aunt Bess, but I imagine that had I known Aunt Bess when I was older I might have found her very interesting . . . no, my house is stacked with books, papers and magazines.[21]

In September 1904, Elizabeth and Agnes' brother Charles was married at Elizabeth's cottage. The autograph book from the wedding contains the signatures of many of Edgewood's residents. Charles, his wife, and their daughter are listed in the 1910 census as living one house from Elizabeth. Charles purchased the Corbett cottage to the north in 1902 and owned it until 1917.

Around 1918, John and Pearl Nelson purchased Elizabeth Abbott's cottage. Mrs. Pearl Nelson was the city nurse for Traverse City; the Nelsons had a home in town on Franklin Street, where they spent the winters. The Nelsons used the cottage as a summer resort boardinghouse and eatery; they opened the "Edgewood Inn" in 1920 and ran it for twenty years. Meals were served to the guests and to the public by reservation. The Nelsons hired Minnie White, a local caterer, to prepare the meals. A July 1928 article in the *Traverse City*

Abbott family at Edgewood. *Seated (l-r)*: unknown, Agnes Abbott, Elizabeth Abbott, Charles Abbott, Barbara Abbott (on floor), unknown, and unknown. *Standing (l-r):* all unknown except for Annie Abbott who is wearing glasses, a white dress, and leaning.

Record-Eagle provided an overview of the Inn.

One of the most enjoyable summer places near Traverse City is Edgewood Inn, a bare two miles out of the city on the Old Mission Peninsula and overlooking the west arm of Grand Traverse bay. "Realizing the routine, the man who wants the greatest possible change from the tiresome noises and crowds of the city, I opened Edgewood Inn," says John S. Nelson the owner. "Its patronage has proven my belief well founded. Fried chicken and fish, the chickens from the back yard and the fish from the front

yard, are the things upon which we most pride ourselves. My wife gives supervision to the preparation of the food. From the fruit and dairy farms about us come the fresh fruits and berries and the clean, wholesome dairy products which are used on our tables. We set a family table."

The Nelsons had continued success with the Edgewood Inn, even through the Great Depression. John Nelson and his wife, Pearl, both died in 1941.

FITZGERALD COTTAGE

James Fitzgerald of Springfield, Illinois, built a "twin" of Elizabeth Abbott's cottage in 1889. According to family legend, Mr. Fitzgerald had passed through Traverse City several times while on business. His ship would anchor in Traverse City and Mr. Fitzgerald fell in love with the area. In September 1888, he purchased a five-acre lot at Edgewood for $450. The family legend is that Mr. Fitzgerald felt the need to stop at the local watering hole for some "courage" before returning home to tell his wife the news of his purchase.

Abbott family *(l-r)*: Charles Left; his wife, Annie, holding their daughter, Barbara; Marjory Abbott; Elizabeth Abbott; Grace Abbott. (circa1907)

Top left: Fitzgerald and Abbott cottages. (circa 1905)
Middle left: Fitzgerald/Stuart cottage. (circa 2005)
Top right: Earl Wsyong. (circa 1939)
Bottom: Abbott / Nelson cottage. (circa 2005)

The Fitzgeralds spent their summers at Edgewood for several years until James's untimely death in 1892. Miss Lucy Lewis leased the cottage from the family for several summers, until Mrs. Fitzgerald and her family returned to Edgewood in the summer of 1896. Three subsequent generations of the Fitzgerald family have enjoyed their Edgewood cottage. One of James Fitzgerald's sons was known to

Left: Mrs. Nora Linane Fitzgerald. (circa 1895)

Below: The children of James and Nora Fitzgerald. (circa 1895)

Top Left: An Apperson Jack Rabbit.

Top Right: Nora Linane Fitzgerald. (circa 1930)

Middle: Betty Wysong and Nora Stuart. (Summer 1939)

Bottom Right: The Stuarts on the beach at Edgewood. (circa 1938)

have brought a car with him on his visits to Edgewood. Mr. Jim Wilson, the son of Margaret (Menauch) Wilson, who was raised by George and Cornelia Lathrop as a foster child, remembered having his first ride in a car:

> . . . there was a guy named Fitzgerald. I had a ride in his car. He lived in Springfield, Illinois, and he had a cottage at Edgewood. They'd put the car on the ship at Chicago and put it off at Traverse City and he'd have it to drive back and forth. As I remember it, the car was an Apperson Jack Rabbit. I tried to find where it was made and I never found any history, but it had across the radiator a big brass rabbit and across the body the name Apperson was written. He didn't think it'd come up the hill from Mathison Road so we had to walk down the road. He took us down to Bowers Harbor and brought us back. That was the first car ride I had . . . probably around 1910.[22]

In later years, the Fitzgerald cottage was nicknamed "The Chip Inn" due to the large chipmunk population in the area. This cottage still belongs to descendants of the Fitzgeralds—it is the only one at Edgewood that still has a direct family tie to the original owner.

Nora Stuart Donn's seventy-fifth birthday party. Edgewood. (July 1995)

CORBETT / ABBOTT / KEEP COTTAGE

Judge Roscoe L. Corbett, a well-known and well-liked local circuit court judge from Traverse City, purchased a large lot on the north end of the Edgewood area and hired local architect Fred Moore (who also designed Frank Hamilton's Sunset Cottage) to design a cottage to be built in the spring of 1898. Judge Corbett was tragically killed in a hunting accident in the Upper Peninsula in November, just a few months after the cottage was finished. His widow, two sons, and a daughter used the cottage until October 1902, when Frank Corbett, the oldest son, and two companions drowned after taking a home-made boat out onto the bay from their Edgewood dock. The bodies of the three boys were never recovered.

Judge Roscoe L. Corbett. (circa 1894)

The Corbett cottage was located eight "doors" north of the Lathrop cottage and was one of the northernmost cottages considered to be part of Edgewood. Mrs. Corbett sold the cottage to Charles J. Abbott in November 1902, just one month after Frank's death. Charles Abbott was the brother to Elizabeth and Agnes Abbott who each owned an Edgewood cottage.

In 1917, Charles Abbott sold the cottage to Wallace and Iva Keep. Mr. Keep had worked for the Pullman Company until he resigned for health reasons. About the same time, the Keeps also bought the Lewis cottages and rented them out, then sold them to the Thirlbys in 1937. The Keeps spent their summers at Edgewood and wintered in Saginaw, Michigan, with family, or in Florida.

Wallace Keep was a distant relative of poet Emily Dickinson. Around 1892, Emily's sister Lavinia, gave Wallace a daguerreotype photo of Emily. He had it in his possession until about 1931, when he donated it to Amherst College. It was the only known image of Emily Dickinson from that time period.

Mr. Keep graduated from Amherst College in 1894 and was a classmate of Calvin Coolidge. In 1926, Mr. Keep, in cooperation with Frank Burkhart, a cherry farmer on the Old Mission Peninsula, and the Fitzpatrick-McElroy theater-chain company, made a cherry pie three feet in diameter and delivered it by automobile to President Coolidge. The entire project was documented in film and still photographs by the Fitzpatrick-McElroy photographer—from the harvesting and processing of the cherries, to the baking and delivery of the pie to the president at his summer home in New York State. The delivery of the pie to President Coolidge was reported in newspapers across the country.

1926 Cherry Festival Queen. Wallace Keep (r).

Mr. and Mrs. Keep used their cottage for many years, sometimes renting it out to others. Mrs. Keep sold the cottage to the Oakes family after her husband's death in 1953. The old cottage was demolished and a modern home was built about 1962. It was designed by the Oakes' son Charles, who was an architect.

SUNSET COTTAGE

Although not actually part of the Edgewood Resort, Sunset Cottage was included in several articles about the Edgewood area. In 1894, Traverse City businessman Frank Hamilton hired local architect Fred E. Moore to design and build a summer home. Sunset Cottage was located on a high bluff about a quarter-mile south of the Lathrop's home. Architect Moore designed a unique feature into the home: he included a stone and brick fireplace and placed the inscription "Sunset Cottage" in the upper part with a sunset scene carved into the stone. Mr. and Mrs. Hamilton used the cottage for seven summers.

L. J. Marks and his wife, Helen, from Chicago, purchased Sunset Cottage in 1906. On June 29, 1909, a fire started in the kitchen and high winds fanned the flames too quickly for Mrs. Marks and her brother to put it out. The home and several out-buildings were destroyed.

Mrs. Marks sold the land to Mrs. Harry VanderVoort of Chicago, who built a new cottage in 1912 and called it "Hilltop." In the 1930s, Harold and Elizabeth Titus bought the home. Mr. Titus was a well-known local author, outdoorsman, and conservationist. Mr. and Mrs. Titus lived in their Edgewood home during the summers until his death in 1967.

Sunset Cottage. (circa 1894)

PHASE TWO: COTTAGES BUILT AT END OF THE LATHROP ERA

Mr. Edward S. Pilsworth dictating criticisms in his studio.

DYE / PILSWORTH / WAKULAT COTTAGE

Local businessman Charles B. Dye and his wife purchased ten acres just to the north of Sunset Cottage around 1912. They built a cottage which they owned for several years. In 1925, they sold it to Mr. and Mrs. Edward S. Pilsworth. Mr. Pilsworth was an English-born artist and the author of three books on early graphic arts as well as science-fiction stories. After Mr. Pilsworth's death in 1937, the home was sold to Mr. and Mrs. Richard Wakulat. In 1941, Mrs. Wakulat sought to supplement the family income by opening a small restaurant inside their Edgewood home. She dubbed it "Pines Inn at Edgewood." She and a good friend ran the restaurant for a couple of years. The Wakulat family lived at Edgewood for nearly sixty years. Richard Wakulat wrote these memories of their beloved home:

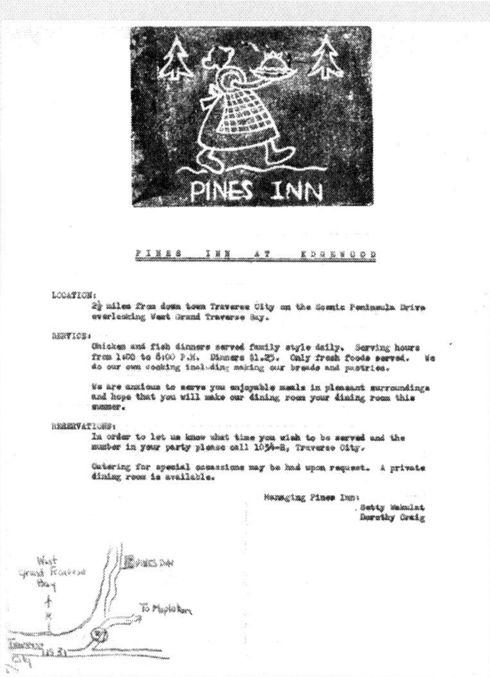

PINES INN

PINES INN AT EDGEWOOD

LOCATION:
2½ miles from down town Traverse City on the Scenic Peninsula Drive overlooking West Grand Traverse Bay.

SERVICE:
Chicken and fish dinners served family style daily. Serving hours from 1:00 to 8:00 P.M. Dinners $1.25. Only fresh foods served. We do our own cooking including making our breads and pastries.

We are anxious to serve you enjoyable meals in pleasant surroundings and hope that you will make our dining room your dining room this summer.

RESERVATIONS:
In order to let us know what time you wish to be served and the number in your party please call 1034-R, Traverse City.

Catering for special occasions may be had upon request. A private dining room is available.

Managing Pines Inn:
Betty Wakulat
Dorothy Craig

Top: Menu from Pines Inn.

Middle and Bottom: Ads printed in the *Traverse City Record-Eagle*. July 1941

Wakulat home. (circa 1937)

Richard and Betty Wakulat with their daughter, Mary Beth. (1948)

"I married not only a beautiful wife but an intelligent and virtuous one. Our common thought was to have a home and some land to breathe in. This we found on our third wedding anniversary. It was an old house on the Old Mission Peninsula on the outskirts of Traverse City, with acreage and frontage on West Bay. It was with love that we purchased the property. It was on this property that we survived the Great Depression and were blessed with two children, a son and a daughter. They had the room to run, play, scamper through the woods, bathe and throw rocks in the bay and the experience of growing a garden not merely for the enjoyment of growing a garden but also with the reasoning that it was important to our very existence . . ."

STONYCROFT COTTAGE

Around 1910, Martin W. Tanner and his wife, Maria, built a small cottage and called it Stonycroft. Mr. Tanner was the owner of a successful dry goods and sporting goods store in Saginaw, Michigan. In his 1931 obituary, Mr. Tanner was described as "a true sportsman, loving the outdoors . . . hunting, fishing, horseback riding, and, in his later years, automobiling . . . when he was 80 years old drove his own car to Traverse City and back." With automobiles still being a novelty to most people, one newspaper article mentioned the Tanners touring the area in their car. Stonycroft remained in the Tanner family until 1947. In the summer of 2005, the cottage was removed from the lot and moved to another location on the Old Mission Peninsula.

GRAYSTONE COTTAGE

In 1902, Mary B. Schryer purchased a small waterfront lot about a quarter mile north of the main Edgewood cottages. With her daughter and son-in law, Walter Dewitt, she built a cottage in 1908 and named it Graystone Cottage. For many years, Graystone and

Left: Obituary photo.

Above: Cartoon of M. Tanner from "A Gallery of Pen Sketches in Black and White of Our Michigan Friend As We See 'Em." by Newspaper Cartoonist Association of Michigan. (1905)

Bittersweet (see page 47) were the only cottages on the waterside of Peninsula Drive. Graystone was also the most northern residence considered to be a part of the Edgewood Resort. "Walter E. Dewitt, of Chicago, formerly with the Kelley Lumber & Shingle Co . . . has erected a very pretty summer home just a little north of Edgewood, the cottage being pleasantly located close to the water."[23]

In 1910, the Dewitts and Mary Schryer were mentioned in the newspaper a few times. "Mrs. Schryer of Graystone cottage was tendered a pleasant surprise Saturday afternoon, the occasion being her birthday anniversary. The Edgewood pioneers gathered

Top: Lee / Bennett cottage. (circa 1981)

Middle left: Stone house built by Wysong family in the 1930s. (circa 2005)

Middle right: Graystone cottage. (circa 2000)

Bottom center: Second cottage built by the Lathrops in 1888. Many additions were added over the years. (circa 2005)

at Graystone and a most pleasant afternoon was spent."[24] "Walter Dewitt has arrived to spend a few days with his family who are summering at Edgewood. Mr. Dewitt left this morning to spend the day fishing …"[25] Graystone was often rented to others when the Dewitts were unable to occupy it. After moving to Wisconsin and spending less time in the area, the Dewitts sold Graystone to Dr. Guy Johnson, a local doctor who used it as a summer home for his family during the 1920s.

> The summer home of Dr. and Mrs. Guy M. Johnson at Edgewood resort, was the scene of a gay Hallowe'en masquerade frolic on Friday evening when their daughter, Joan, delightfully entertained thirty of her friends. The rooms throughout the cottage were prettily decorated with Hallowe'en symbols, corn stalks, Jack O' Lanterns, black cats and witches vying with each other for the places of prominence. The children joyously participated in the games and contests which had been arranged for their pleasure, the party concluding with delicious refreshments served by Mrs. Johnson. [26]

The Johnsons sold Graystone cottage around 1928 and moved to California. It has had several owners since then.

LEE / BENNETT COTTAGE

In 1904, Fred Lee of Chicago built a summer home on the lot to the north of the Fitzgerald's cottage. Not much is known about Mr. Lee or exactly when his cottage was built. He is only briefly mentioned in two articles in 1906 and 1907.

In 1909, he sold the cottage to Anna "Nannie" Bennett, the daughter of Civil War Cavalry General R. H. G. Minty and Grace Abbott (the sister of Elizabeth, Charles, and Agnes Abbott). In 1911, Mrs. Bennett, who was now widowed, had plans in place to open a dining hall across the road from her cottage, naming it "The Lismore." However, Mrs. Bennett died suddenly after surgery in February 1912, and the dining hall was never completed past the foundation. Her young daughter Charlotte and two older, grown children had no interest in the Edgewood cottage. The property was re-possessed by the bank and sold in 1914. Over the years, it has been owned by several families. In 1999, the old cottage was torn down and a new home constructed in its place.

WYSONG COTTAGES

After the passing of Cornelia Lathrop in 1912, the Wysong family purchased one of the small cottages built by the Lathrops in 1888. The cottage was located just to the north of the Lathrop home and it became part of the Wysong gravel pit land. Miss Ruth Wysong lived and worked out of the home as bookkeeper and secretary for her brothers who ran the gravel operation. The cottage was changed dramatically by the Wysongs, with fieldstone being added to the outside of the cottage and several additions, including a kitchen. A large fieldstone fireplace took up an entire wall at the back of the cottage. Behind that was a kitchen and the upper floor was turned into a dormitory.

According to a family member, Ruth Wysong opened the cottage to visiting actors who were performing at the Cherry County Playhouse at the Park Place Hotel in Traverse City during the 1950s and early 1960s. Ruth kept a guest register with the signatures of many famous actors who came to Traverse City during that time. She also owned the guest book from the Edgewood Inn run by the Nelsons in the 1920s and 30s. Early in the 1960s, Miss Wysong moved into another small cottage on the gravel pit property. Ruth and her niece were killed in a tragic car accident at Edgewood in 1973. Sadly, the guest registers that Miss Wysong had kept so proudly have been lost since her death.

Jay P. Smith wrote a column titled "The Observer" for the *Traverse City Record-Eagle.* It appeared regularly during the 1920s through the 1950s. Below is the column from May 6, 1953:

A June day along the Edgewood shore.

There was a time for you.

From far across the water came the drone of the "big mill."

That, the sound of little waves nibbling at the sandy shore, and the sweet tones of the song sparrow, were the only things to break the great fragrant silence of the summer day.

A three-masted schooner comes lumbering slowly up the bay before a light breath of air and another sail is visible about half down over the horizon off the point of Marion Island.

Two gulls wheel slowly, high overhead with as little exertion as one of the fleecy white clouds, about as big as your hand, lazy just like us.

The whole world is lazy. Even a bumblebee softens his bumble as he wings heavily from a bluebell to a tiger lily near the shore.

We watch the bluebells or harebells nodding up and down toward the southeast like a Mohammedan bowing toward Mecca.

The June silence is shattered by a terrific screeching chatter and an angry kingfisher comes flying in empty-billed, and lights on a dead pine branch where he sits and pouts, his head rumpled up and ragged.

What a day to lay on the warm sand still cool from winter cold and not yet warmed by summer heat, with your hands over your eyes to protect them from the sun.

There's nothing wrong anywhere in the world. People live peacefully and in contentment.

A sand piper comes fluttering in and lands running. He hustles along the shore and every time he stops his little tail bobs up and down. No wonder they call them Teeter Bottoms.

Nothing mars the day. Nothing is out of harmony.

We've had lots of days like that.

But they were fifty years ago.

IN CLOSING

THE Edgewood community of the late nineteenth and early twentieth centuries was a close-knit one. The residents shared social activities and helped each other during good times as well as bad. For many of the Edgewood resorters who returned each year, the summer was akin to an annual family reunion.

Beginning with the death of Mrs. Lathrop in 1912, the original cottage owners began to pass away and changes started to take place. With the deaths of Harriet Bacon in 1916, Lucy Lewis in 1918, Agnes Abbott in 1920, and Elizabeth Abbott in 1925—all single women with no children to inherit their cottages—the Edgewood pioneers were gone. The "glue" which had held the resort community together had come apart.

By the late 1920s, most of the cottages were privately owned, with many of them being rented out during the summer months and kept vacant in the winters. The larger properties were split up and more homes were eventually built on both sides of the road. Once the cottages were no longer a resort community, and instead became private summer and year-round homes, the resort atmosphere faded, although the name remained familiar to a few local residents.

The research for this story has helped current Edgewood residents meet each other and become aware of the history of their homes. Also descendants of the Lathrops, Abbotts, and other early Edgewood residents and visitors have visited the area to see where their ancestors spent their summers. The original Edgewood owners would probably be happy to know that their homes have been preserved for more than a century and are enjoyed by the current owners as much as they were in the 1890s. Even with all of the construction on the Old Mission Peninsula, a bit of Traverse City resort history still lives on, in these old homes and through the people who helped put this story together.

Edgewood Resort may no longer exist, but it is remembered through vintage postcard images, photographs, newspaper articles, and the stories that have been preserved here.

NOTES

1. *Grand Traverse Herald.* May 17, 1894.

2. *Grand Traverse Herald.* June 23, 1898.

3. *Grand Traverse Herald.* June 1894.

4. *Traverse City Record-Eagle.* July 25, 1911.

5. *Grand Traverse Herald.* June 21, 1894.

6. *Grand Traverse Herald.* June 20, 1895.

7. *Traverse City Record-Eagle.* July 28, 1911.

8. *Ibid.*

9. *Grand Traverse Herald.* August 3, 1893.

10. *Grand Traverse Herald.* September 8, 1892.

11. *Traverse City Evening Record.* July 18, 1908.

12. From an interview with James Wilson, *Memories Hidden Memories Found on the Old Mission Peninsula.* Julianne Myer, editor and interviewer. 1994

13. *Traverse City Record-Eagle.* June 12, 1911.

14. *Minty and His Cavalry: A History of the Saber Brigade and Its Commander*, Rand Bitter. 2006, pg. 501.

15. *Traverse City Evening Record.* September 14, 1920.

16. *Ibid.*

17. Bernard Flickinger shared this information with the author during an interview. Mr. Flickinger's father told the story. Bernard Flickinger still lives in the area known as Edgewood. This story was also confirmed by Mrs. Rhea Sivek, who spent her childhood summers at Bittersweet Cottage.

18. "A look at local industry. No. 37. A series sponsored by Oleson's Food Stores of Traverse City," *Traverse City Record-Eagle*. November 24, 1962.

19. *Grand Traverse Herald*. July 1894.

20. Around 1940, Mr. R. Daggett was killed on this section of the road and in 1973, Ruth Wysong and her niece were killed in an auto accident at Edgewood.

21. Excerpt from a letter written by Charlotte Bennett Blair, cousin of Barbara Abbott whose parents were married at Edgewood in 1904. The letter was donated by Barbara Abbott's daughter Mary Ellis.

22. From an interview with James Wilson, *Memories Hidden Memories Found on the Old Mission Peninsula*. Julianne Myer, editor and interviewer. 1994

23. *Traverse City Evening Record*. July 3, 1908.

24. *Traverse City Evening Record*. June 27, 1910.

25. *Traverse City Record-Eagle*. July 10, 1910.

26. *Traverse City Record-Eagle*. October 30, 1924.